Me and Willie and Pa

Tad Lincoln

Me and Willie and Pa

The story of Abraham Lincoln and his son Tad

by F. N. Monjo

Illustrated by Douglas Gorsline

Simon and Schuster
New York

Text copyright © 1973 by F. N. Monjo
Illustrations copyright © 1973 by Douglas Gorsline
All rights reserved
including the right of reproduction
in whole or in part in any form
Published by Simon and Schuster, Children's Book Division
Rockefeller Center, 630 Fifth Avenue
New York, New York 10020
SBN 671-65211-7
Library of Congress Catalog Card Number: 73-11464
Manufactured in the United States of America

3   4   5   6   7   8   9   10

Dedicated to the memory of
Annie S. Proctor,
who told me the first story I ever heard
about
Abraham Lincoln

1860-1861

WHEN I look back, thinking about our time in Washington, most everything I remember is sad. That's not the way me and Willie supposed it would be—not when our Pa was President and all. But then, we never reckoned with that long, long war, nor with a heap of other things besides.

First off, back in Springfield, Illinois, when Pa heard he was nominated, he was tickled. So was Mama. And so was my big brother Bob. And me and Willie, we was real tickled, too.

I wish you could have seen those torchlight processions at night going past our house on Eighth Street—all the marchers wearing their "Wide-Awake" capes and caps, holding up their kerosene torches, hollering for Pa. Everybody singing

Old Abe Lincoln
Come out of the wilderness . . .

Once there was six thousand people marching past. That parade took two hours and a half just to get past our house.

Folks called him "the Rail Splitter," and they carried big signs saying

Honest Old Abe
the Rail Splitter
for President!

And they loved him, too. Because he had been born poor like most everybody else, in a log cabin, and he was tall and bony, and he talked kind of plain and slow and easy, and he was patient and kind, and he'd just as soon stop whatever he was doing and tell jokes to anybody who'd listen.

Here's a joke he told me once.

"Tad," says Pa, "how many legs would a calf have if you was to call his tail a leg?"

"Well, Pa, he'd have *five*," I said.

"No, son, he wouldn't," says Pa. "He'd have just four. Calling a tail a leg won't *make* it a leg."

And I had to laugh at the way he'd fooled me. Pa sure could be fun.

Me and Willie and Mama was at home when Pa heard he'd got enough votes to be President. Pa had been over at the telegraph office waiting for the returns to come clicking in over the wire. Soon's he knew it was all over, he came straight home, and said to Mama, "Well, Mary, We're elected."

Our house, on Eighth Street, in Springfield

And Pa sat down and looked like he wasn't going to say one more word about all this election commotion that was turning the world upside down.

"Mr. Lincoln," said Mama, "I declare you are the most closemouthed person in this world! You must tell me all about it! You must give me all the details!"

Mama never could get Pa to gossip about things or to brag on himself, no matter how hard she tried.

Pretty soon the whole crowd came over, and our house was full of people, all congratulating Pa because he'd just got to be the sixteenth President of the United States.

My big brother Bob asked Pa, "Ain't you beginning to

11

Mary Todd Lincoln

Abraham Lincoln

Sarah Bush Lincoln, my grandma

get a *little* tired of this constant uproar?" He meant all the fuss and confusion of campaigning.

I don't know about Pa, but you can just bet me and Willie loved every minute of it. That, and what came next.

You know what Pa used to call me and Willie? He called us his dear codgers, sometimes. Or rascals. Or his blessed fellows. Mama said Pa started calling me Tadpole, or Tad for short, when I was a baby. Pa said I looked just like a tadpole with my big head and my skinny legs. But my real name is Thomas.

Thomas Lincoln, my grandpa

Just before we left Illinois for Washington, Pa went out to the farm to say goodbye to my grandma, Sarah Lincoln. She's real old, and Pa was afraid she might not live much longer. She's Pa's stepmother, and she and Pa loved each other a heap. Pa said she used to help him with his studies. And he said Grandma always used to say she knowed young Abe was going to be a great man some day.

On February 11, the day before his birthday, Pa stood up there on the last car at the end of the train in Springfield saying goodbye to the folks 'cause we was leaving for Washington.

Gorsline

"I now leave, not knowing when or whether ever I may return," Pa said. Then he bid them an "affectionate farewell," and the train pulled out.

Mama and all us boys traveled on that train to Washington along with Pa and lots of his friends. When we had got as far as Indianapolis, Pa fussed some at my big brother Bob 'cause he thought Bob had lost the satchel that had his inauguration speech in it. But Bob found the plaguey speech later on, and everything turned out all right.

At every town we went through, crowds came down to the train to see Pa. He'd tell them he hoped there wasn't going to be a war, but if there *was* a war, they'd better fight hard for the Union. Not for *his* sake, Pa would tell them, but for their own sakes. 'Cause the Union was the best thing all us Americans was ever going to have in our whole lives. Now and in the future, world without end.

Sometimes me and Willie would play jokes on people in the crowd. They'd all keep hollering, "Show us Long Abe! Show us the Rail Splitter!"

"You want to see Old Abe?" we'd holler back. "Well, *there* he is!" And then we'd point out Judge Davis or Mr. Ward Lamon, both of them just as short and fat as could be. Just the opposite of Pa, 'cause Pa was as skinny as one of them rails he used to split, and he stood six foot four.

Our train went all through Ohio and across New York State. When we got to New York City, Ma and Pa took me and Willie to P. T. Barnum's Museum to see all the freaks

We saw three midgets and a giant at Barnum's Museum

they had there. And another day me and Willie went to Laura Keene's Theater, while Mama and Pa went to a big reception at the Astor Hotel.

When we got down to Philadelphia, folks were saying there might be some trouble when our train went through Baltimore, because people thought Maryland might go secesh and quit the Union and start rioting any minute. So Bob and Pa went through Baltimore at night, and Mama and me and Willie came through the next day. But we all got to Washington safe.

While Mama was in New York, she went shopping at

Lord and Taylor's and Stewart's, and all the other big stores, buying silks and velvets and other dress goods, and gloves and lace, and furniture and china and curtains for the Executive Mansion, and I don't know what all. Pa used to get kind of disgusted with all that shopping. He said all that stuff cost too much, and it was nothing but flubdub anyway.

But Mama said she was *not* going to have all the ladies in Washington laughing at her for being some kind of backwoods countrywoman from way out west on the Illinois frontier with no nice clothes. And if she was going

Willie and me, with Mama

to be First Lady, she was going to have some pretty dresses. And you bet she *had* some, too!

Pa sure found a mess when he got to Washington. All during November, December, January, and February, that old fool, President James Buchanan, had just been sitting there watching while seven states went secesh.

A state goes secesh when it says it's going to quit the Union. Pa said couldn't *any* of them quit the Union, no matter what they claimed. But just the same, me and Willie knowed that South Carolina, Mississippi, Alabama, Georgia, Florida, Louisiana, and Texas had already walked out. And old Buchanan never raised a finger to try to stop them. He was leaving all the hard work for Pa.

Here's what Mr. Horace Greeley printed in his newspaper, the New York *Tribune,* about those secesh states. "Let the erring sisters depart in peace!" said Mr. Greeley.

Pa said that was foolishness and humbug. Every one of those states would *have* to come back in, Pa said. But Pa knew if he tried to force them, there'd surely be a war.

When they swore him in as President, Pa told the South he wasn't going to be the one to start a war. If they wanted a fight, Pa said, the South would have to start it. Pa said, "We must not be enemies."

Well, by jings, if one month later South Carolina didn't go and start it up themselves, by firing on Fort Sumter!

Despite all that, for about a year me and Willie had the time of our lives in Washington. My big brother Bob was away at college, at Harvard, studying to be a lawyer like Pa.

Me and Willie had a pair of pet goats, and a cat, and a

*The dome of the Capitol was still unfinished when Pa was
inaugurated in 1861*

Tad Lincoln in his Zouave uniform

dog named Jip, and we had ponies to ride. And Willie
had a set of tracks and trains. We had Bud and Holly
Taft to come over and play with us nearly every day. And
we built a fort for ourselves, with wooden cannon, up on
the flat roof of the Executive Mansion, to scare away the
Rebels.

Sometimes we made Mama's servingmen stand sentry
duty as guards for our army. Bud and Holly Taft and me
and Willie had our *own* army, I mean. We all had uniforms. We called ourselves "Mrs. Lincoln's Zouaves."
(A Zouave is a soldier who wears a red cap, a blue jacket,
and baggy red pantaloons.) Willie was the colonel. Bud
was the major. Holly was the captain. And I was the drum
major.

22   I had a big soldier doll, too. He was dressed up like a

Bud and Holly Taft

Zouave, and his name was Jack. He was just a private. Sometimes Jack would turn out to be a spy, and we'd have to hang him and then bury him in the rose garden. The gardener said we was ruining his flowers burying Jack all the time.

One time, Jack deserted. That meant he was going to have to be shot. But me and Willie went to Pa—he was right in the middle of a cabinet meeting—and I got Old Abe to write me out a pardon for him:

> The doll Jack is pardoned,
> by order of the President.
> A. Lincoln

Pa didn't care if I called him "Old Abe." He'd just smile that smile.

Sometimes he'd come up to the attic if Bud and Holly and Willie and me was putting on a circus or a minstrel show. We'd charge him five cents admission. One time I sang him a song:

> Old Abe Lincoln,
> A rail splitter was he,
> And he'll split
> the Confederacy. . . .

Pa looked real serious. He said it might take a long time to split the Confederacy. 'Cause Pa had had four more states go secesh on him as soon as Sumter was fired on, and the war started, and Pa called for volunteers. Soon as that happened, Virginia, Arkansas, Tennessee, and North Carolina had walked out too.

Pa was afraid he might lose Missouri and Kentucky and Maryland besides. But they never *did* go secesh, as it turned out.

I felt mighty sorry for Pa, those days—not getting to be President of the *whole* Union, and him loving it so much. I mean, after he won his election, all fair and square, and then him getting to be President of only *half* of the country!

I guess that was part of the reason Pa's face used to

look so sad sometimes. Some folks said he was ugly.

Looked like a gorilla, they claimed. Well, he never looked ugly to *me*.

The folks who said those things about Pa must never have seen him smile.

Remember I was telling you about Jack, the Zouave doll? Well, Willie and me knew a *real* Zouave. He was Colonel Elmer Ellsworth. Pa said he was "the greatest little man" he ever met.

He had come to study law with Pa back in Springfield, and he'd traveled to Washington on the train with us when Pa got to be President. He was here at the Executive Mansion so much that when me and Willie caught the measles, in March, Colonel Ellsworth caught them too.

He was one of the first to be killed in this war. He led some troops into Alexandria, Virginia, and he was shot dead hauling down a Rebel flag.

Pa told them to hold Ellsworth's funeral right here at the Mansion, and Pa and Mama and Willie and me, every one of us cried.

They let me keep the flag that Elmer Ellsworth captured. I still have it to this day.

I can't tell you about all the killing and all the battles there were in this war. It went on for four long, horrible years, and hundreds of thousands of young fellows died—just like Elmer Ellsworth. All I can do is tell you some of the things I remember best. And don't blame me if they're not all jokes. I told you, most of it's sad.

I also got to tell you about a big, whopping bunch of defeats. Because about all Pa had, for three years there, was a whole procession of bad generals and bad defeats.

The first one was Bull Run. Bull Run is a creek, a little way down in Virginia, not far from Washington. The newspapers and everybody'd been hollering, "On to Richmond!"

(Richmond's where the Rebs had their capital, and where Jeff Davis was.)

Col. Elmer Ellsworth

Gen. P. G. T. Beauregard, CSA

General McDowell told Pa his troops was too green to take Richmond yet.

"You are green, it is true," said Pa, "but *they're* green also. You are *all* green, alike." I guess Pa figured we wasn't any greener than the Rebs was.

Well, the Army marched into Virginia, and a lot of foolish ladies and gentlemen from Washington came along after them in their carriages, to watch. As if they was going to a picnic in the country.

Only instead, the Rebs—General Beauregard and General Stonewall Jackson—sent the whole shootin' match piling back into Washington, with all those folks' carriages clogging up the roads and everybody hollering and shrieking all along the retreat.

Pa was so disgusted with that defeat that he got rid

of General McDowell right away and put in General

McClellan in his place. The soldiers called him "Little Mac." But he wasn't much good either.

I'm not going to try to tell you about all the soldiers and generals that was in and out of Washington when we was there. Seemed like every time me and Willie looked up, there was some plaguey general, asking some favor of Pa—just when we was about to start playing marbles with him, or Pa was fixing to spin our tops.

And the waiting rooms was just bulging with people begging Pa for jobs—jobs in ministries in Europe, or jobs in some post office here in this country—or asking Pa to make them officers in the Army. Always something pokey like that. Pa was patient and kind with everyone, but he couldn't help them all.

He joked about it once. Pa said all these people begging him for jobs, while the other half of the country was in rebellion, made him feel like a man busy renting out rooms in one half of his house while the other half was on fire.

That first summer in Washington it got so hot and tiresome, Mama decided to do a little shopping in Philadelphia and New York, and then she said we'd go on and spend some time at the seaside, in Long Branch, New Jersey. Me and Willie and Bob went along, and so did Pa's secretary Mr. Nicolay, and Mama's cousin Lizzie Grimsley, and Mama's friend Mrs. Shearer.

Sea bathing is lots of fun for boys, but I don't know how ladies *stand* it. We boys just got into our suits and

Bathing machines

went on into the water. But the ladies had to get all dressed up from head to foot in long wool bathing dresses and caps, and then they had to sit down inside of these bathhouses on wheels — they called them "bathing machines" — and then the whole bathhouse, with them inside, was lowered down the beach, on tracks, with a windlass! And when the whole bathhouse was lowered into the water, the ladies would get out and kind of slosh around some. Now, I don't call that fun!

After that we went to Niagara Falls, and to Saratoga, and we were back in Washington in September.

Pa sure was glad to see us. So was Mary Ann Cuthbert, Mama's housekeeper. And John Watt, the head gardener. And Edward McManus, the head doorkeeper. And Mama's dressmaker, Elizabeth Keckley.

Mama calls her Lizzie. But I couldn't say my *l*'s so good, so I just called her Yib.

Yib once used to sew dresses for Mrs. Jefferson Davis—but that was long before Jeff Davis became the Rebel president, down there in Richmond.

A few weeks after we got back to Washington, poor Yib heard that her only son, George, had been killed fighting for the Union, in Missouri. She was heartbroken, and she put on black, for mourning.

Yib Keckley

1862

Willie Lincoln

I DON'T really remember too much about Christmas that first year—in '61—because I was only eight and a half. But I sure did remember that next February, in 1862.

First, I better tell you that Willie was Mama's favorite. He was always just as good as pie. He loved to go to church, and be good every kind of way. Mama thought maybe he'd be a minister someday. When we'd go to church on Sundays, Willie'd sit there just as quiet while the minister prayed and prayed for Pa.

"I don't see why preachers pray so *long* for Pa," I'd say.

"Well, Tad," Pa would answer, "I suppose it's because

the preachers think I need it. And I guess I do."

Anyway, Willie went out riding on his pony one day in the rain, and he got sick with a real bad cold, and spite of everything the doctors could do, he just couldn't get better. Bud Taft came over to be with him and comfort him. But on the twentieth of February, Willie died.

I'd been sick myself, and had to be in bed, and Yib Keckley made black clothes for Mama and me, and she sewed black armbands for Bob and Pa. I didn't think Pa was ever going to smile again. He said Willie was too good for this earth—"but then, we loved him so."

And then he looked at Mama and said, "Mother, try and control your grief, or it will drive you mad." But Mama just cried and cried and cried.

I cried a lot too, but that didn't do Willie any good, or Ma or Pa either. Mama couldn't bear to see Bud and Holly Taft anymore, 'cause they made her think of Willie. And I sent away Willie's toys and trains, 'cause they made me think of him too.

About this time, we heard that someone way out west, on the Cumberland River in Tennessee, had captured the Rebel Fort Donelson. His name was General U. S. Grant.

But Pa's General McClellan sure hadn't done much in Virginia. He just *wouldn't* move. Pa said if General McClellan didn't want to use the Army, Pa would like to borrow it himself!

In March, '62, the ironclad ships *Monitor* and *Merrimac*   33

Pa visited Gen. McClellan in his tent, down in Virginia,
and asked him to get on with the war

had their battle. And a little after that, General McClellan
finally made a move on Richmond. But their new Rebel
general, named Robert E. Lee, beat him back, in May.

After Willie died, I couldn't sleep so good. Me and Willie,
we used to sleep together. So Pa told me anytime I couldn't
get to sleep, I could come to his room. Sometimes I'd
slip down the corridor, past the sentry on duty there,
and crawl into bed with Pa.

One night when we was in bed, going to sleep, a Con-
gressman came right into Pa's bedroom and asked him to

pardon a soldier who'd been sentenced to death the next morning, for going to sleep on duty.

"Well, I don't believe shooting will do him any good," said Pa. "Give me that pen."

That summer of '62, when it got hot, we left Washington and went out to stay at the Soldiers' Home for a while. It was on the Maryland side, a few miles out of the city, and it was cool and pleasant there.

Pa kept hoping General McClellan would give him a big victory. You see, Pa wanted to free the slaves, but Pa's Secretary of State, Mr. Seward, said he shouldn't do it until after he had had a solid victory and it began to look like the North could really win the war.

'Stead of a victory, Pa had another defeat that summer, at the Second Battle of Bull Run.

And in September, General Bobby Lee and his Confederates came roaring up into Maryland.

"Little Mac" McClellan got his hands on a copy of Lee's battle plans. (Don't ask me how he got them.) Even so, he couldn't smash Lee. Best he could do was mostly hold Lee to a draw, at the Battle of Antietam. And after it was over, "Little Mac" didn't even try to chase the Rebs back across the Potomac. Even after Pa sent him a telegram about Lee, saying, PLEASE DON'T LET HIM GET OFF WITHOUT BEING HURT.

Pa was fit to be tied.

Even though Antietam was almost a draw, Pa said he

Soldiers killed in the battle of Antietam

just could claim it was a victory. I told you how he needed that victory real bad because he wanted to issue his advance notice of an Emancipation Proclamation.

Now, isn't *that* a jawbreaker?

That's what they called it, though. It was a paper Pa wrote declaring all the black folks free. Everybody who'd been a slave, anywhere in the Rebel South, well, Pa was going to set them free.

There was black folks weeping and crying "Hallelujah!" for joy that day all over Washington. Yib Keckley, too. And I reckon there was plenty black folks giving thanks, and crying, lots of other places I didn't see.

This was September 22, you understand. And this Emancipation Proclamation paper wasn't supposed to take effect until January 1, 1863. But still, Pa wanted to put everybody on notice of what he meant to do.

I told Pa I didn't understand much about emancipation.

"Tad," said Pa, "let me explain it to you the way Petroleum V. Nasby does."

Pa could remember whole stories, right out of his head. If Pa liked something, he said, it just seemed to stick.

Anyhow, Petroleum V. Nasby is one writer Pa really loved. The V is for Vesuvius. Pa would just sit there chuckling over the comical sayings of this ignorant old countrified preacher, supposed to hail from Wingert's Corners, Ohio—him and his wife, "Looizer Jane, the pardner uv my buzzum."

Pa said, "Petroleum V. Nasby heard that down South

A slave cabin, down South

they was saying how good slavery was, because the black folks was weak and the white folks was strong, and wasn't it kind and right for the strong to take care of the weak?"

"Well," Pa said, "Petroleum V. Nasby said that was *such* a good idee that he was going to introduce it to the members of his church congregation, in Ohio. So he set up a little contest, a weight-lifting contest, to see who was strong enough to lift six hundred pounds and who was too weak to do it. Old John Podhammer could lift the weight easy. But William Sniffles couldn't.

"'Well, Willyum,' sez Old John, 'since you can't lift that six hundred pounds, from this time henz4th, and furever, you air my man. An ez you have more furniture

A young Confederate

than befits yer lowly condishen, I will send a team over tomorrer, and take yer bureau and bedsteads up to my house . . .'

"Then in comes Mrs. Sniffles, who kin lift six hundred pounds *easy,* even with Old Podhammer on top of it! And it was no time afore she diskivvered what his bidniss wuz.

"She turned red in the face. Said she:

"'You goin' to take my furniture?'

"'Certingly.'

"'And we air your slaves?'

"'Uv course.'

"'And you kin sell my children?'

"'Naterally.'

"'You old beast!' shreekt the infuriated female. 'You sell my babies, you take my furniture, drat ye, I'll give ye some of it *now!*'

"Whereupon she hurled a chair, which laid Old Podhammer flat on the floor. Then she picked him up and flung him out the door."

Pa was real comical telling me about it, and I had to laugh.

"And then, old Petroleum V. Nasby ends up that story, Tad," said Pa, "by saying 'The experiment, for the present, hez the appearance of a failure.' You see, *nobody* wants to be owned by somebody else, Tad. And if slavery isn't wrong, *nothing* is wrong."

I never forgot it.

"Little Mac" McClellan

Well, the first of November, in '62, Pa got rid of "Little Mac" McClellan, 'cause he still hadn't started to move South again after Robert E. Lee. Mama said McClellan was a humbug. Pa said, "He had the slows."

Pa put in General Burnside, but six weeks later, *he* had a horrible defeat at Fredericksburg. So Pa pulled him out and put in "Fighting Joe" Hooker in his place. Pa sure was having trouble finding a good general!

The head of all the Southern armies, Gen. Robert E. Lee

I believe it was around then some fellow asked Pa how he liked being President. And Pa said it reminded him of the man who'd been tarred and feathered and was being rid out of town on a rail. Pa said the fellow on the rail said, "If it wasn't for the honor of the thing, I'd just as soon walk!"

Pa sure was serious about keeping this Union together, though, even if he *did* joke about it. Like that story he used to tell about Blondin.

Did you ever hear of Charles Blondin? He's a French acrobat who's crossed Niagara Falls a couple of times on a tightrope! That's one thousand one hundred feet across, and he was a hundred and sixty feet above the water. He *made* it, too.

Well, one time some fellows from out West came to see Pa, trying to give him some free advice about how to win the war.

Pa listened patient, for a while. Then he spoke up and said:

"Boys, if I was Blondin, and I had everything valuable you owned strapped to my back, and I was fixing to cross Niagara Falls on a tightrope, would you stand there, shakin' the rope, sayin' 'Blondin! Look out, there! A little more to the left! Wait, Blondin! A little more to the right!' You would *not*! You'd stand back, real quiet, and you'd let me try to get across the best way I knew how!"

By jings, that was how Pa told them to quit worrying

44 him and let him save the Union the best way he could.

Charles Blondin, the tightrope walker

Mama was always worried that Pa was going to be killed by an assassin. Pa said there was no use to worry: Anybody real set on killing him could always kill him, unless he was to live shut up inside an iron box. And then how could he be President? So I worked out a code with Pa, for when he was locked up working in his office, so's he'd know it was me and not some assassin. It was three short knocks and two long. Dot, dot, dot, dash, dash. And he'd always open.

Pa had two private secretaries, Mr. Nicolay and Mr. Hay. Mr. Hay didn't know I knew it, but he had some nicknames for Pa. He called him "The Tycoon" some-

Harriet Beecher Stowe

times, and sometimes "The Ancient." He had a name for Mama, too. He called her "The Hellcat." Well, Mama *has* a high temper, and she was mighty jealous of Pa!

Mr. Hay said when Pa looked at you with those gray eyes of his, it felt like Pa was seeing clear through you to the buttons on the back of your coat.

I wish you could have seen some of the people who came to the Executive Mansion to meet Ma and Pa.

One of them was Harriet Beecher Stowe. She wasn't young or pretty. She was skinny, and she wore her hair kind of frizzy. She said she'd come to Washington to go to a Thanksgiving dinner given for about a thousand slaves who'd run away from the South. And she wanted to see Father Abraham (that's what folks commenced calling Pa) to make sure that Pa's Emancipation Proclamation was a "reality and a substance, and not a fizzle out of the little end of the horn."

Pa told me she was the lady who wrote *Uncle Tom's Cabin* — that book everybody read, about how Simon Legree used to whip his slaves, and about Little Eva, who was kind, and about Eliza, the slave girl, and her baby, running away from slavery, chased by bloodhounds across the ice on the Ohio River.

Pa told me Mrs. Stowe's book made folks hate slavery worse than they ever had hated it before. When she came to see him, he bent down to shake hands with her. Then Pa smiled and said, "Is this the little woman who made this great war?"

Another visitor was Mr. Frederick Douglass. He was a tall, powerful black man who ran away from being a slave, in Maryland, many years ago. He had sons of his

Frederick Douglass

own fighting in the Union Army, and he was mad at Pa because he said the black soldiers wasn't being treated equal with the white soldiers.

Pa said he knew that was true, but he couldn't put everything right all in one day, and someday the black soldiers *was* going to be treated right, and he hoped Mr. Douglass would trust him to hurry that day along. And Mr. Douglass said he would, and went away to help raise some more black troops for the Union.

Someone else who came there was a lady named Julia Ward Howe. She wrote the words to that marching song the soldiers love to sing, "The Battle Hymn of the Republic."

You should have seen Pa's face—tears running down his cheeks—when he was standing in a window reviewing the troops going off to war. The men would be marching through the night, by torchlight, tramping down Pennsylvania Avenue, singing that song:

Mine eyes have seen the glory of the coming of the Lord.
He is trampling out the vintage where the grapes of wrath are stored.
He hath loosed the fateful lightning from his terrible swift sword.
His truth goes marching on.
Glory! Glory! Hallelujah!
Glory! Glory! Hallelujah!
Glory! Glory! Hallelujah!
His truth goes marching on!

1863

Julia Ward Howe

WHEN New Year's Day, 1863, came, Ma and Pa gave a big reception. Pa stood there in his white kid gloves shaking hands with people for hours and hours.

About three o'clock in the afternoon, he stepped out of the line and went to his office, where there was about a dozen gentlemen waiting for him. Mr. Seward, the Secretary of State, and his son Fred handed Pa the paper. Then Pa signed the Emancipation Proclamation. And about three and a half million slaves became free men.

We heard that one-hundred-gun salutes was fired off that night in Pittsburgh, and Buffalo, and Boston, when the newspapers printed Pa's proclamation, and in some cities there was all-night meetings, with folks cheering and singing, and lots of black folks praying and crying and blessing Pa.

So Mrs. Stowe didn't have to worry. It didn't turn out a fizzle after all.

General and Mrs. Tom Thumb

At one of Ma and Pa's big receptions, there came a little midget and his little midget wife. Their real names was Mr. and Mrs. Charles Sherwood Stratton, but everybody called them General and Mrs. Tom Thumb. Pa introduced me to them.

P. T. Barnum, the big showman, is their manager. He shows them off to folks all over the country. Mr. Barnum used to say, "There's a sucker born every minute." But General Tom Thumb and his wife sure was *real* midgets, and no fraud about it. They had to stand up on a sofa to talk to Pa!

The war kept grinding along just as bad as ever. "Fighting Joe" Hooker lost a great big battle, in May, at Chancellorsville, Virginia. And we heard that the Rebel General Stonewall Jackson was killed there—shot by accident by one of his own men.

Then, after a while, General Hooker asked to be relieved, and Pa put in General Meade in his place.

Gen. "Stonewall" Jackson

A few days after that, on July 2, Mama was driving out to our summer place, at the Soldiers' Home. The horses ran away with her, and she had to save herself by throwing herself out of her carriage. She hurt her head real bad, and she had to be in bed for three weeks.

Right while Mama was sick, me and Bob and Pa heard that there was a terrible big battle being fought up in Pennsylvania, between General Meade and General Lee, at a place called Gettysburg.

Our side won, after a ghastly four-day fight. But Bob said Pa just wept when he heard General Meade hadn't been able to chase after the Rebs, and catch their whole army, before they crossed back over the Potomac and got away safe to Virginia.

"If I had gone up there, I could have whipped them myself," said Pa.

One thing made him happy, though, and that was the news from Vicksburg, Mississippi. Vicksburg was the last big stronghold the Rebs had on the Mississippi River, and General Grant captured it, on July 4 — the same day Gettysburg was being fought. Pa said General Grant must be some fine general.

"I can't spare *this* man," said Pa. "He fights."

Pa knew I was crazy about uniforms and soldiers, so sometimes he'd walk downtown with me to Stuntz's toyshop and buy me some lead soldiers and brass cannon that would really shoot.

Gen. Ulysses S. Grant

Sometimes Mama and Pa would go out driving in an open barouche, and I would ride along beside them on my pony. Many times we'd see a bearded fellow with pale, serious eyes, like a prophet from the Bible, staring after us. I used to wonder who he could be.

Walt Whitman, the poet, sometimes saw the Lincolns when they went driving

I was always glad when summer came, because they'd send my tutor away and I wouldn't have to study for a while. I sure hated books and reading. Mama was worried about that and tried to *make* me study. Pa would just smile and shake his head and say, "Let him run. There's time enough yet for him to learn his letters. And get pokey."

I know Bob thought Pa spoiled me rotten. You can bet Yib Keckley thought so too. But half of the time when I was bad, I just did what I did to help keep Pa from looking so sad—thinking about Willie, and the war.

Me and Pa used to walk from the Executive Mansion over to the War Department every night, so Pa could read the telegraph dispatches and keep up with the news from the armies in the South.

Pa used to tell me that the War Department belonged to Mr. Stanton. Mr. Stanton was Pa's Secretary of War. Pa would say, "Tad, you better behave, now, when we go over to Mr. Stanton's." Pa had a nickname for Mr. Stanton. He called him Mars. And he had a nickname for Mr. Welles, his Secretary of the Navy. He called him Neptune.

Well, one night when we was at the War Department, I drew some funny faces in India ink on the top of a big marble table they have there. I guess I got kind of inked up myself. And the clerk sure did get steaming mad at me!

But Pa just laughed, took me by the collar and led me home.

"You know I don't amount to pig tracks in the War Department, Tad," said Pa. Then he grinned at me. "And after this scrape, neither will you!"

Mama took me and Bob up to New Hampshire for a couple of months that summer, to the White Mountains. And when we was coming back to Washington, in September, we got a telegram from Pa saying there'd been another Union defeat, in Georgia. At a place called Chickamauga.

Mama's brother-in-law was killed there. He was a

This is Mama's sister, my aunt Emilie Todd Helm

Rebel general named Ben Hardin Helm, married to Mama's sister, my Aunt Emilie.

Three of Mama's brothers died fighting for the South, besides Ben Hardin Helm. And some folks was mean enough to say that Mama was a rebel herself. But that was all lies. Mama was every bit as loyal to the Union as Pa.

If I hadn't got so sick that fall, with scarlatina, Mama and I could have gone up to Gettysburg with Pa. But I was sick in bed, and Mama had to stay in Washington to nurse me.

On November 19, 1863, Pa spoke a little speech at

57

*Every American, North and South, remembers what Pa said
at Gettysburg*

Gorsline

the cemetery they was dedicating to the thousands of poor fellows who had got killed there back in July. Pa's speech was only ten sentences long. Here's how it ended:

. . . we here highly resolve that these dead shall not have died in vain; that this nation, under God, shall have a new birth of freedom, and that government of the people, by the people, for the people, shall not perish from the earth.

Not much before Christmas that year, my Rebel Aunt Emilie Helm and her little daughter, my Rebel cousin Katherine, come to the Executive Mansion. Mama and Pa used to call Aunt Emilie their "Little Sister."

I nearly had a fight with cousin Katherine one night when all of us, Mama and Pa and Aunt Emilie and me, was sitting in front of the fire and I was showing Katherine an album of pictures. We came to a picture of Pa.

"And there's the President," I said.

"No. Jeff Davis is President," said Katherine.

I hollered, "Hurray for Abe Lincoln!" and she hollered, "Hurray for Jeff Davis!"

But Pa took both of us into his lap and said, "Tad, you know who is your President. And I'm your little cousin's Uncle Lincoln."

You remember I told you Katherine's daddy, Ben Hardin Helm, was killed at Chickamauga?

Well, that made Mama sad, and she said, "Kiss me, Emilie, and tell me you love me."

And Pa said, "You know, Little Sister, I hope you do

Jefferson Davis

not feel any bitterness, or that I am in any way to blame for all this sorrow."

Then Pa put his arm around Aunt Emilie, and both of them cried.

Aunt Emilie told Pa she was worried about Mama. Aunt Emilie said Mama told her that Willie's ghost sometimes come to visit her. Pa knew all about that. He knew Mama liked to go visit spiritualists—people who would pretend they could call up spirits from the dead. Pa said they made Mama believe that she was really talking to Willie. So Pa worried about her too.

61

1864

Gen. U. S. Grant

THERE was so much sadness during that war, it's good to remember something happy.

One of the happiest days I remember was the day Pa made General Ulysses S. Grant the leader of all the armies of the Union. After he took Vicksburg, Pa knew General Grant was an absolutely number one, first-rate soldier. So next thing you know, Pa moved him over to Chattanooga, Tennessee, and let him straighten things out over there. Pretty soon, he was into Georgia.

General Grant left his right-hand man, General Sherman, down there in north Georgia, pounding his way south towards Atlanta. And Pa brought General Grant up here to Washington so's he could try to take Richmond.

Mrs. Julia Grant, his wife, said she knew her husband could do it, 'cause he was "a very obstinate man."

He was short, with ginger-colored hair and blue eyes, and he seemed like a mild little fellow, kind of quiet and ordinary-looking. But Pa said he was like a bulldog, and if anybody could take the South by the throat, *he* could.

Mama said Grant was just a butcher. And there's no denying that an awful lot of soldiers did get killed when General Grant was in command. But Pa got kind of irritated with Mama, and he said if she knew so much about it, maybe *she* should go down there and lead the armies. Mama didn't say another word.

The day Pa put General Grant in charge, there was a whole mob of people in the East Room. Grant's son, Fred, was with him, too. Fred Grant got to tag along with *his* pa all through the war. Wasn't that something?

With all those people staring at him, and shaking his hand, General Grant commenced blushing like a schoolgirl. He had to wipe sweat off his face when Pa gave him his commission. And then folks hollered, "Stand up where we can have a look at you," and Grant stood up on a sofa so's everyone could see him.

A little while after that, Grant plunged into Virginia, and by the end of July he had Richmond and Petersburg under siege.

It was around that time that Pa had his Secretary of War, Mr. Stanton, give me a commission as colonel. A full colonel, in the Army! Colonel Tad Lincoln, with a uniform and everything. My big brother Bob was furious when he heard Pa was spoiling me so, and letting me post guards anywhere I wanted to around the Executive Mansion. But Pa just let me be, no matter how Bob fussed.

Bob wanted to enlist himself, but when Mama heard

63

Ruined factories in Richmond, Virginia

Caroline

Gen. William Tecumseh Sherman

about it, she cried and begged Pa not to let him go. She said she had already lost one son, and didn't dare lose another. Pa told her *lots* of other folks were losing their sons, but he finally gave in to her, and Bob went back to Harvard.

On September 2, 1864, General Sherman wired Pa from Georgia:

ATLANTA IS OURS, AND FAIRLY WON.

A little while later, he burned the factories and public buildings there, and half the rest of the town went up in flames with them.

That victory in Atlanta made it pretty certain that Pa would win the election—because that fall he was up for reelection, come November.

Some people said General Grant might try to get the nomination and run for President, but Pa said he knew General Grant would never give up the siege of Richmond until he'd licked the Rebels. When Grant heard what folks was saying, he laughed and said he didn't *want* to run for President. He said the only office he wanted, when the war was over, was to be mayor of his hometown, Galena, Illinois. And when he *got* to be mayor of Galena, he was going to do one thing sure: get that sidewalk fixed twixt his house and the railroad depot.

Pa said he knew all along that that was what Grant would do.

A Confederate soldier

Guess who *did* run against Pa, for the Democrats? "Little Mac" McClellan—the general Pa had had to get rid of, 'cause he had the slows.

Well, Pa won easy. And a magazine run this cartoon of him, saying "Long Abe, a little longer," 'cause they thought Pa was going to be around for four more years as President. But it didn't turn out that way.

Along about the middle of November, all news from General Sherman, down in Georgia, stopped coming in over the wires. Pa had no idee where he and his armies was. "I know the hole he went in at," said Pa, "but I can't tell you what hole he'll come out of." But all of us knew that Sherman had said, "I can make Georgia howl."

"Long Abe, a little longer."

Turned out that Sherman and his army—marching in a column sixty miles wide—had cut theirselves off from their supplies and commenced living off all the hogs and chickens and cornmeal they could find on all those Georgia plantations. Sherman had learned how to do that from General Grant, 'cause that's what *he'd* done, down at Vicksburg. And Sherman's men marched from Atlanta to Savannah—all the way to the sea—burning houses and barns, and tearing up railroads, and freeing slaves in droves.

In December of that year, Sherman sent another telegram to Pa, saying:

I BEG TO PRESENT YOU, AS A CHRISTMAS GIFT,
THE CITY OF SAVANNAH.

Pa answered him right back:

MANY MANY THANKS FOR YOUR CHRISTMAS GIFT.

'Cause Pa and everybody else knew, after Savannah, that the South couldn't last much longer.

1865

Gen. and Mrs. Ord, and daughter

END OF January, beginning of February, we heard that Sherman's armies was in South Carolina — where the Rebels first fired on the flag. And we heard that the cities of Charleston and Columbia was going up in flames.

Everything seemed to fold up pretty quick after that. There was still plenty of hard fighting, but we knew we was going to win.

When Pa was inaugurated President for the second time, March 4, 1865, the Capitol dome rose up perfect and beautiful, soaring up into the sky. Four years earlier when he stood there, taking the oath the first time, it had been only half finished.

While Pa spoke, the sun came out from behind the clouds, and Pa told the South that he was speaking "with malice toward none, with charity for all."

You see, to Pa's way of thinking, all those secesh states

never *had* got out of the Union at all, no matter what *they* thought.

A few weeks after that, at the end of March, General Grant invited me and Mama and Pa to come down and visit him in Virginia. He said the war was almost over.

We traveled down Chesapeake Bay to where he was, at City Point, Virginia, on a steamship called the *River Queen.*

Mrs. Grant and all her children was there, too.

By that time, my brother Bob was finished with Harvard, and he'd been made an officer on General Grant's staff.

On March 27, Pa had a war conference with Admiral Porter, and Sherman, and Grant, on board the *River Queen.* When they asked Pa what he calculated he was going to do about the South soon as we won the war, Pa said, "I want to let 'em up easy."

Little while after that, Pa was reviewing some troops alongside of the wife of one of General Grant's generals. They rode along on horseback. Her name was Mrs. Ord, and she was real pretty. When Mama heard about it, she was red in the face. Jealous! Screaming at Pa. Right out in front of everybody. Mrs. Ord started to cry.

Pa never said a word.

Pretty soon after that, Mama went back to Washington. But I stayed there, with Pa.

Admiral Porter asked me and Pa to spend the night on board his ship, the *Malvern.* Admiral Porter lengthened

Gorsline

Tad Lincoln in his colonel's uniform

When Pa and me had our picture taken by Mathew Brady, Brady gave us a big album to look at, and Pa said he hoped folks wouldn't think he was making out he was reading me the Bible

Jefferson Davis' children, Jefferson, Billy, and Margaret,
with William Howell, and their servant, Robert Brown

our bunk on the ship so's Pa could have enough room to
stretch out and be comfortable.

On April 3, 1865, we heard that Jeff Davis and General
Lee and his army had finally had to run. The city of
Richmond had fallen!

Parts of it was still burning when me and Pa went in.
We drove around the city in a carriage that day, saying

howdy to all the hundreds and hundreds of black folks

*Some called the house where Mr. and Mrs. Jefferson Davis lived
in Richmond, Virginia, "the Confederate White House"*

who wanted to see Abraham Lincoln, the man who had
set them free.

On April 4, we went to the Confederate White House,
where Jefferson Davis had lived all through the war. Pa
sat at his desk for a minute or two, but he never said a
word.

There's a big, high two-story porch out behind that
house, and a brick walk down beneath it. They told us that

Me and Pa

Jeff Davis' little boy—they called him "Little Joe"—had fell off that porch, playing, and killed hisself on the walk below, just about a year earlier. When that happened, Jeff Davis must have felt just like Pa did when Willie died.

We all went back to Washington after that, and as soon as we got home we heard that General Grant had caught up with the Rebel army. General Lee had had to surrender at Appomattox. And the war was over.

There was people crying and cheering in Washington, and bells ringing, and fireworks, and bonfires in the streets.

On Monday afternoon, April 10, Pa spoke to thousands of people who'd come to the Executive Mansion to holler and cheer for Father Abraham and for the end of the war. Pa saw they had a band with them. So at the close of his talk, he said he was going to ask that band for some music. Pa said he wanted them to play one of the best tunes he had ever heard.

You know what he asked for? It was "Dixie."

Pa told the folks, "It's Federal property now."

Tuesday evening, April 11, there was a big torchlight review of the Army. Pa spoke to the soldiers, and to the rest of the crowds, from an east window of the Executive Mansion.

One time, years before, when Pa was speaking to the troops like that, I hung Colonel Ellsworth's Rebel flag out

Gorsline

Pa looked young and happy before the war began

When it was over, he was tired and sad

Folks listening to Pa speaking, once the war had finally ended

of the window and waved it back and forth. Pa didn't mind, that time, 'cause he knew where I'd got the flag. And he knew I waved it just to cheer him up with my foolishness.

But this night, I didn't do anything as foolish as that. I just stood behind Pa, at the window, while he read his speech to the soldiers. As he spoke, he handed me the pages he'd finished, one by one.

Pa said, "We meet this evening not in sorrow, but in gladness of heart. No part of the honor or praise is mine. To General Grant, his skillful officers and brave men, all belongs."

But every one of us standing there knew we'd never of won without Pa.

Every time before some big battle, Pa used to have this terrible dream. He'd dream he was sailing in a fast, fast ship about to crash on a dark and distant shore. And he dreamed that dream again that week. But he couldn't imagine why, because Lee had already surrendered.

The afternoon of April 14, Mama and Pa went for a carriage drive. Mama said Pa was happy. The war was over at last, and they could look forward to a trip to Europe.

And Pa said he'd like to see California, too.

He recited some lines for Mama from a poem he loved called "Resignation," by Henry Wadsworth Longfellow.

There is no flock, however watched and tended
    But one dead lamb is there!
There is no fireside, howsoe'er defended
    But has one vacant chair . . .

He told Mama they'd been too unhappy, because of the war and Willie. And now he was going to make it all up to her, and they would have some rest, and some peace. Pa said, "We must be more cheerful."

Ford's Theater, Washington, D.C.

John Wilkes Booth

That same Friday night, April 14, Mama wanted to see a play. She and Pa went to Ford's Theater with some friends to see Laura Keene in *Our American Cousin.*

My tutor and I went to a different theater that night ourselves. We went to see *Aladdin, or the Wonderful Lamp,* at the National. My brother Bob and John Hay stayed at the Executive Mansion, having a talk upstairs.

When my tutor and I got home from *Aladdin,* lots of strange people came crowding up to our carriage. They were crying and calling out to us. At first, we couldn't make out why they were there or what they were saying. Then somebody hollered out Pa had been shot. Another fellow said he was dead.

I didn't find out what really happened to him until sometime the next morning. They told me Pa died at 7:22 A.M.

By then it had started to rain. And even bigger crowds of black folks, and white folks too, had come to stand outside on the lawn, in the drizzle, and weep for what had happened to Pa.

They told my grandma, Sarah Bush Lincoln, back in Illinois, what had happened. She said, "I knowed, when he went away, he'd never come back alive."

And Mama cried and cried and cried, and nobody could stop her. Yib Keckley was crying. And so was I. And so was Bob. And everybody else who was there.

It seems this actor, John Wilkes Booth, shot Pa and hollered something. Then Booth jumped to the stage and ran into the alley behind the theater and rode away on a horse. And they haven't been able to catch him yet. They say Booth was more than half crazy, but that he must have thought he was helping the South.

But Pa had said he'd "let 'em up easy." So how could Booth have thought he'd be helping the South? How *could* he have shot him?

How could anyone want to hurt my Pa?

About This Story

AMERICANS will never be able to think of Abraham Lincoln in a dry, factual manner. But the dry facts of his personal life are as follows: he was born, on February 12, 1809, in a log cabin on the south fork of Nolin Creek, near Hodgenville, Kentucky, the son of Thomas Lincoln — a poor backwoods farmer and carpenter — and Nancy Hanks Lincoln, who was probably illegitimate. Neither of his parents had had any formal education whatever. He had a sister, Sarah, two years older than he, who died in 1828, and a brother, Thomas, who died an infant. His mother died when he was nine years old, and on December 2, 1819, his father married a widow with three children. Her name was Sarah Bush Johnston.

Sally Bush Lincoln (or "Sairey," as she was sometimes called) must have been one of the kindest stepmothers in the history of the world. She wouldn't let anyone ridicule or "hinder" ten-year-old Abe when he was learning his letters, writing in charcoal on the back of a wooden shovel, or lying in front of the open fire in their cabin reading the books he had borrowed. Many years later she said she had always known he was going to be a great man, and she sent him "a heap" of love. They loved each other dearly all their lives.

The Lincoln family moved from Kentucky to Indiana and then to Illinois. In New Salem, Abraham split rails, worked in a grocery store, managed a mill, worked as a surveyor, eventually taught himself law, and in 1836 was licensed as an attorney. In 1842 he married Mary Todd, whose father was a wealthy banker and slaveholder from Lexington, Kentucky.

Lincoln served one term in Congress, 1847–49, and opposed the policies of Senator Stephen A. Douglas of Illinois, a Democrat, in the early 1850's. He joined the Republican Party in 1856, when it was formed. In 1860, as a moderate opponent of slavery, he won the Republican nomination for the Presidency and then the national presidential election.

As the sixteenth President of the United States, he was our leader all during the Civil War, which he brought to a victorious conclusion. The preservation of the Union and the freeing of the slaves were the two overwhelming achievements of his administration.

In freeing the slaves when he did, Lincoln was helping to bring the South — albeit against its will — into the modern world. For long before the United States freed its slaves, most of the nations of South America (with the exception of Brazil) and all the nations of Europe (with the exception of Russia, where the serfs were not freed until 1860) had done away with serfdom and slavery. So it was not only inhumane for the South to cling to slavery as desperately as she did, but also hopelessly backward and behind the times, for slavery had been doomed in the court of world opinion thirty years prior to 1863.

Lincoln was shot five days after Lee's surrender, on

the evening of April 14, 1865, by the actor John Wilkes Booth, and died at 7:22 the next morning. Booth (1838–65) was a demented man who had been plotting the President's assassination for six months. After a two-week search by the Army and the Secret Service, he was found in a barn near Bowling Green, Virginia. The barn was burned; Booth was shot trying to escape and died soon after.

Lincoln had four sons:

Robert Todd Lincoln (August 1, 1843–July 26, 1926) was the eldest. He graduated from Harvard and became a lawyer. He served as Secretary of War under Presidents Garfield and Arthur and was Minister to Great Britain under President Benjamin Harrison. From 1897 until 1911 he was president of the Pullman Company. He married Mary Eunice Harlan (the daughter of Senator James Harlan of Iowa) on September 24, 1868. They had a son and two daughters: Mary (or "Little Mamie," born October 15, 1869), Abraham ("Jack," born August 14, 1873), and Jessie Harlan Lincoln (born November 6, 1875). "Jack" Lincoln's early death on March 5, 1890, before he was seventeen, ended the possibility of the continuation of the Lincoln name.

Lincoln's second son, Edward Baker (born March 10, 1846), didn't live quite four years. He died February 1, 1850, in Springfield.

His third son, William Wallace ("Willie"), was born December 21, 1850, and went to Washington when Lincoln became President. Willie was not much more than

Tad Lincoln at seventeen

eleven when he died, in the White House, on February 20, 1862, to the terrible grief of both his parents.

Lincoln's favorite was unquestionably his youngest son, Thomas, nicknamed "Tad." Tad was born April 4, 1853, in Springfield. Willie and Tad spent one very happy year in the White House (1861–62), but after Willie's death Tad's life was naturally much sadder than it had been before. The lonely little boy was a very bad student, read poorly, could scarcely write, and spoke with a pronounced lisp or speech defect. His mother, and especially his father, spoiled him unashamedly — probably because Willie was no longer there.

After his father's death, Tad's life grew still more somber. His widowed mother, who had grown increasingly unsound mentally, imagined herself to be in deep financial difficulties. Nevertheless, on October 1, 1868, she sailed with Tad to Europe, where she put him in school in Frankfurt-am-Main, Germany — living in a hotel there herself, so that she could be near him. They visited the Austrian Tyrol, England, Scotland, and Baden. They did not return to New York until May 11, 1871, and then went to Chicago, where Tad developed "a severe cold." (Nobody is sure what was wrong with Tad, though it has been suggested that he and perhaps all his brothers, his nephew, "Jack," and his father as well may have suffered from the Marfan syndrome, a hereditary disease caused by a genetic defect, which is often accompanied by asymmetrical growth, eye trouble, and cardiac disease.) Whatever his illness, he died on July 11, 1871, in Chicago, three months after his eighteenth birthday.

In 1875, Mary Todd Lincoln's mental problems grew so acute that she had to be confined for some months in a private sanitarium in Batavia, Illinois. At her sanity hearing, her surviving son, Robert, was obliged to testify that his mother had been of unsound mind since the death of his father. Adjudged capable of managing her own affairs in 1876, she spent the next four years traveling in Europe. She died in Springfield on July 16, 1882.

This story, of course, does not include these later unhappy events, but confines itself to the four years (1861–65) when Lincoln and his family were living in the White House — or the Executive Mansion, as it was then termed. It is written as if Tad had witnessed and recorded it all. While he might have seen and heard nearly everything told here, he actually left no written record of his life in the White House with his unforgettable Pa.

Bibliography

The American Heritage Pictorial History of the Presidents of the United States by the editors of *American Heritage.* American Heritage Publishing Co., New York, 1968.

The American Heritage Picture History of the Civil War by the editors of *American Heritage,* with narrative by Bruce Catton. American Heritage Publishing Co., New York, 1960.

Tad Lincoln's Father by Julia Taft Bayne. Little, Brown, Boston, 1931.

Artemus Ward: His Book by Charles Farrar Browne. Carleton, New York, 1862.

Artemus Ward's Best Stories by Charles Farrar Browne. Harper, New York, 1912.

The Everyday Life of Abraham Lincoln by Francis Fisher Browne. Putnam, New York, 1915.

Tad and His Father by F. Lauriston Bullard. Little, Brown, Boston, 1915.

Wit and Humor of Abraham Lincoln by Carleton B. Case. Shrewsbury, Chicago, 1916.

A Diary from Dixie by Mary Boykin Chesnut. Appleton, New York, 1905.

Narrative of the Life of Frederick Douglass, an American Slave by Frederick Douglass. Harvard University Press, Cambridge, Mass., 1960.

Health and Disease by René Dubos and Maya Pines. Time-Life Books, New York, 1965.

Mrs. Abraham Lincoln by W. A. Evans. Knopf, New York, 1932.

Lincoln: A Picture Story of His Life by Stefan Lorant. Harper, New York, 1957.

The Nasby Papers by Petroleum Vesuvius Nasby (nom de plume of David Ross Locke). Perrine, Chicago, 1864.

A Short Life of Abraham Lincoln by John G. Nicolay. Century, New York, 1902.

Lincoln's Sons by Ruth Painter Randall. Little, Brown, Boston, 1955.

Julia Ward Howe by Laura E. Richards and Maud Howe Elliott. Houghton, Mifflin, Boston, 1916.

Abraham Lincoln: The Prairie Years and The War Years by Carl Sandburg (one-volume edition). Harcourt, Brace, New York, 1954.

Life and Letters of Harriet Beecher Stowe by Harriet Beecher Stowe, ed. by Annie Fields. Houghton, Mifflin, Boston, 1897.

Mary Todd Lincoln: Her Life and Letters by Justin G. Turner and L. L. Turner. Knopf, New York, 1972.